More **SOUTHERN STEAM** - South and West

MORE SOUTHERN

STEAM - SOUTH AND WEST

TONY FAIRCLOUGH AND **ALAN WILLS**

D. BRADFORD BARTON LTD

Frontispiece: A Channel Islands boat train at Woking, 14 August 1965. Nine Elms shed has rostered the pioneer 'West Country' Pacific, No. 34001 *Exeter,* for the turn.　　　[G. D. King]

© Copyright D. Bradford Barton Ltd ISBN 085153 211X

Published by Enterprise Transport Books Ltd
3 Barnsway, Kings Langley, Hertfordshire WD4 9PW

Printed and bound in Great Britain by BPC Hazell Books Ltd

introduction

The services operating out of Waterloo have, for many
years, ranked among the most important in the country.
During the Southern Railway's existence the suburban
lines were electrified and gradually the third rail was
extended outwards to reach such centres as Reading and
Portsmouth, giving these areas excellent communications
with the capital. But the long distance trains to the South
and West of England remained in the hands of steam
power and it was not until July 1967 that the last regular
steam-hauled expresses to and from London ceased to
run. Thus, many enthusiasts maintained an affection for
the Southern Region which, until the mid-'sixties, could
provide the sight of steam engines, both ancient and
modern, at work in and around the capital. Because of the
emphasis on electrification, many of the older designs
originating from the drawing offices of such locomotive
engineers as Adams, Drummond, Urie, Maunsell and
Bulleid, together with the Riddles 'Standards', were still
earning good revenue well into the Nationalised era. It is
hoped that the photographs in this volume, which is a
sequel to *Southern Steam South and West,* will recall to
mind many of these old favourites going about their daily
tasks. First, the reader is taken down the main line from
Waterloo to Basingstoke, then on to the Weymouth,
Bournemouth, Southampton, Salisbury and Portsmouth
areas, with views included of many of the wayside stations
and branch lines which have been closed and are now but a
memory.

The 12.00 noon Waterloo to Lymington Pier boat train provided interesting motive power over a period of many years. When a batch of 'Schools' 4-4-0s arrived at Nine Elms in the 1960s, they found their way on to the turn on summer Saturdays, and some fine performances were recorded. No. 30937 *Epsom* seen at Waterloo in August 1962, was one of the 21 members of the class fitted by O. V. Bulleid with Lemaitre blastpipe and large diameter chimney, a modification which seemed to have little significant effect upon the performance of the engines.　　　　　[G. D. King]

Steam power had but a few more weeks to work when 'Battle of Britain' 4-6-2 No. 34052 (formerly *Lord Dowding*) was photographed moving away from the great terminus at Waterloo with a Basingstoke semi-fast in the summer of 1967. The engine is in splendid external condition, a credit to its home shed of Salisbury.   [G. D. King]

A typical platform-end scene at Waterloo on 1 April 1958. Bulleid light Pacific No. 34011 *Tavistock* has been fully coaled in preparation for its 171-mile run to Exeter with a West Country express while Salisbury shed's famous 4-6-0, No. 30453 *King Arthur* makes the prescribed cautious entry into the terminus with an up express. The start for heavy expresses from Waterloo was not easy for the drivers of the light-footed Bulleid Pacifics, as the steam sanders could not be used for fear of disrupting the track-circuiting equipment.

[A. R. Butcher]

A parade of veteran motive power at Waterloo on 25 July 1951. 'M7' 0-4-4T No. 676 has been acting as empty stock pilot, while the Urie 'N15' 4-6-0 has recently arrived with an up express. The middle locomotive No. 30119, was the most famous of Drummond's 'T9' 4-4-0s, as was the engine generally used for light-weight Royal Trains.
[P. J. Lynch

Drummond engines active at Waterloo on 4 May 1957. 'T9' 4-4-0 No. 30338 poses close to 'M7' tank No. 30243, which has steam up for a stint of carriage shunting at the terminus.
[A.E. Bennett

Maunsell designed the 'W' Class 2-6-4 tanks in 1931 for freight work in the London area, but No. 31924 is seen performing empty stock working at Vauxhall in August 1962. These three-cylinder tanks had 5ft. 6in. wheels but were rarely, if ever, used on passenger turns.   [G. D. King]

Urie built the five massive 'H16' 4-6-2Ts for heavy transfer freight turns from Feltham shed, but on busy summer Saturdays they were pressed into service as motive power for empty stock workings between the carriage sidings at Clapham and Waterloo. Nos. 30517 and 30519 have excited the interest of youthful train spotters at Waterloo on 8 September 1956.
[G. D. King]

The L.S.W.R. built a large locomotive depot at Nine Elms, some two miles out from the terminus near Vauxhall station. Coded 70A in BR days, the depot had an allocation of over ninety engines in the 1950s, while visiting engines from Salisbury, Exmouth Junction, Basingstoke, Eastleigh and Bournemouth were serviced before returning to their home stations. This line-up of engines outside the 'new' shed includes No. 30861 *Lord Anson,* one of Maunsell's 'Lord Nelson' 4-6-0s with which the depot was always associated.

[D. T. Cobbe]

The *doyen* of the 'Nelsons', No. 30850 *Lord Nelson* roars through Raynes Park with the 11.30 a.m. Waterloo to Bournemouth on 2 October 1957. This was an Eastleigh Top Link turn, worked by the men who had come up to Town with the 7.22 a.m. from Southampton.   [A. R. Butcher]

A smaller Maunsell engine, 'U' Class 2-6-0 No. 31634, hurries past the same spot with a semi-fast for Basingstoke. At that time (October 1957) the third rail took electric trains as far as Brookwood; beyond that point, steam reigned supreme. [A. R. Butcher]

The big 4-6-0s designed by Drummond in the early 1900s were expensive failures. When Robert Urie succeeded as C.M.E. in 1912 his first task was to produce a reliable heavy mixed traffic engine. The result was the first 'H15', numbered 30482 in BR stock, which is seen running past Surbiton on the down through road on 22 March 1957. Nos. 482 to 491 were always known as the 'Chonkers', a nickname which suited them admirably.

[A. R. Butcher]

Another world-famous Salisbury engine, No. 34051 *Winston Churchill,* speeds through the suburban station of Earlsfield, five-and-a-half miles out from Waterloo, on 1 April 1958.

[A. R. Butcher]

16   An up Bournemouth express, hauled by No. 34090 *Sir Eustace Missenden,* is turned off the main line on to the up local at Farnborough in August 1965. The civil engineers had complete possession of the fast line between Farnborough and Brookwood in order to instal the third rail for the electrification of the route. Drivers had to exercise extreme care when negotiating these sharp cross-overs, the temporary speed restrictions often being quite severe.

[G. D. King]

When Maunsell assumed command as C.M.E. of the newly formed Southern Railway in 1923, he wisely adopted and improved existing designs which were already basically sound. Among these was Urie's 'N15' 4-6-0, and in 1925, the first of the new engines, No. 453, emerged from Eastleigh Works. The improved locomotive had a higher boiler pressure at 200lbs. per sq. in., but, more significantly, long-travel valves. The publicity department came up with the wonderful idea of naming the engines after characters in the Arthurian legend, and so *King Arthur* was born! The engine went new to Salisbury shed after its early trials and remained there until its withdrawal in 1961, by which date it had completed over two million miles of running. This fine revenue-earner is seen racing past Byfleet with the 8.15 a.m. from Salisbury to Waterloo on 20 May 1949.

[D. T. Cobbe]

Nos. 34040 *Crewkerne* and No. 31639 await departure from Farnborough with down trains, 7 September 1957.　　[Hugh Davies]

Another highly successful Maunsell improvement on a Urie design was his 'S15' 4-6-0. Very similar to the 'King Arthurs', these engines had 5ft. 7in. wheels and proved excellent mixed traffic machines, handling the Southern's heaviest freight turns as well as helping out with holiday reliefs in the peak traffic periods. No. 30830, built for £10,415 in 1927, had only two more months of service ahead when it was caught by the cameraman at the head of a down freight at Brookwood, 15 May 1964. This engine spent its working life at Salisbury, amassing one-and-a-quarter million miles of hard running.

[P. J. Lynch]

19

Morning activity at Winchfield, between Farnborough and Basingstoke, in May 1960. A down local, hauled by 'L1' 4-4-0, No. 31753 has called at the station, while a special with 'King Arthur' 4-6-0 No. 30791 *Sir Uwaine* at its head, roars by on the down through road.

[Derek Cross]

Another 'Arthur', No. 30796 *Sir Dodinas le Savage* leaves Winchfield in the up direction with the 8.46 a.m. Salisbury to Waterloo, 12 August 1961.

[D. T. Cobbe]

No. 30788 *Sir Urre of the Mount* heads 'up the local' away from Basingstoke with a parcels train from Southampton, 17 April 1957. Although their best work was performed on express trains, the 'Arthurs' worked many useful miles on such turns as this.

[A. R. Butcher]

The up road from Basingstoke, 17 April 1957. Bournemouth 'King Arthur' No. 30782 *Sir Brian* is signalled away on to the Reading line with the Bournemouth to Birkenhead through train; the fireman is busy shovelling coal forward for the next leg of the journey to Oxford, where the Southern engine will come off, to be replaced by a Western 4-6-0 for the remainder of the run.

[A. R. Butcher]

An 'S15' 4-6-0, No. 30510, clumps westwards along the down local line towards Basingstoke with a mixed freight, 17 April 1957. These Urie engines were based at Feltham shed and ran most of their mileage on heavy freight rosters.   [A. R. Butcher]

Following the success of the 'Chonkers', Urie modified the 'H15' design with a tapered boiler, and ten engines, of which No. 30475 is an example, were built in 1924. These locomotives were at their best at such hard-slogging jobs as this up parcels from Southampton terminus, seen leaving Basingstoke in September 1960. [Derek Cross]

Shorn of its nameplates, No. 34088 still looks an impressive machine as it stands under the fine gantry at the eastern end of Basingstoke station, 14 August 1965. The lefthand signal, in the 'off' position, indicates that the train will be turning off the up London road and taking the Reading line to the western Region.   [G. D. King]

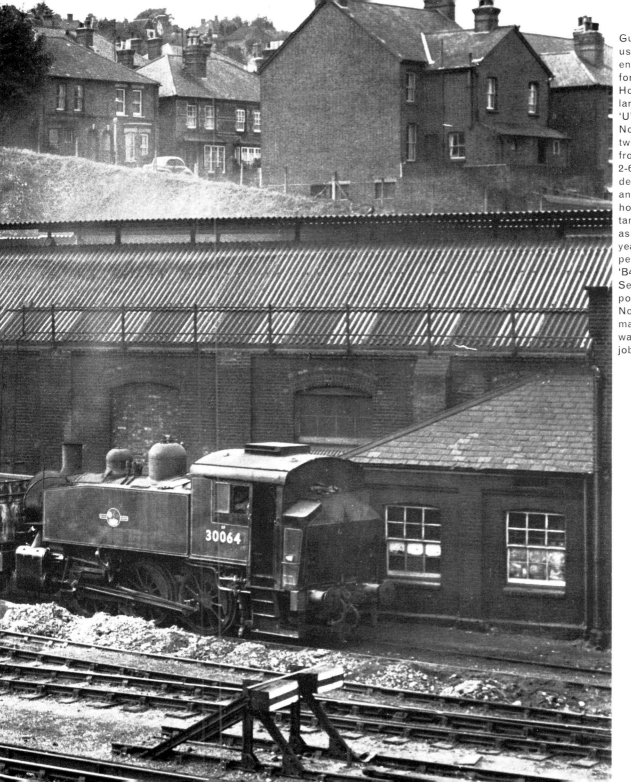

Guildford shed (70C) usually had some fifty engines on its allocation for working around the Home Counties, the largest of which were its 'U' Class Moguls. No. 31799 was one of twenty 2-6-0s, rebuilt from Maunsell's 'K' Class 2-6-4Ts in 1927. The depot had a straight shed and an open roundhouse, for which a small tank was retained to act as shed pilot. For some years this work had been performed by an Adams 'B4' 0-4-0T but by September 1964, the powerful 'USA' 0-6-0T No. 30064, immaculate in malachite green livery, was in residence for the job. [P. J. Lynch]

25

The Adams '395' Class 0-6-0s, introduced by the L.S.W.R. in 1881, were built by Neilson and Co. of Glasgow for £2,430. No. 30575 was almost at the end of its 75 year career when it was photographed at Guildford in June 1958. These fine old engines were used as yard pilots and pick-up goods engines during BR days.
[Peter Winding]

This general view of Guildford station shows 'N' Class 2-6-0 departing with a train for Redhill in 1962. The London services were electrified, but steam worked numerous cross country passenger and freight turns in the area.   [G. D. King]

The Bulleid 'Q1' 0-6-0s were considered ugly by most connoisseurs of locomotive design, yet they were very efficient freight engines, and although not 'star attractions', it is possible to consider them Bulleid's most successful design. No. 33015 takes coal at the coal stage of its home shed, Guildford, on 23 May 1964.
[J. R. Besley]

Standard Class '4' 4-6-0 No. 75070 takes it steadily around the curve at Ash Junction with a Reading to Guildford parcels train in the summer of 1962. The single line is the route down to Alton and on 'over the Alps' to Winchester. [G. D. King]

As the last Maunsell 4-6-0 left in service, 'S15' No. 30837 achieved considerable fame in its final months of service, often working special trains to numerous destinations. The engine makes a brave sight against the snow-covered countryside near Alton with an LCGB 'S15' Commemorative Rail Tour on 16 January 1966. [D. M. Cox]

The same tour was also hauled by 'U' Class 2-6-0 No. 31639 down the Bentley to Bordon line. This Mogul has acquired one of the taller Standard-type chimneys in place of the Maunsell original. [D. M. Cox]

The line to Weymouth opened on 20 January 1857, with trains arriving from the broad gauge system via Yeovil and from London via Southampton. The Southern developed its passenger services from Waterloo to Weymouth and eventually took over the entire boat train workings to the Channel Islands via Weymouth in 1959. Rebuilt 'Merchant Navy' 4-6-2 No. 35001 *Channel Packet* starts away with a London-bound express, 2 July 1961.

[K. A. Stone]

Up trains face a long hard pull from Weymouth to the summit near Upwey, the stretch through the station being at 1 in 51. Many trains required banking assistance in order to clear this section in the time allowed. 'West Country' No. 34006 *Bude* has a light load behind the tender on 29 July 1962.

[K. A. Stone]

Another up express clears the precincts of Weymouth station behind modified 'West Country' 4-6-2 No. 34104 *Bere Alston* on 29 July 1962.

[K. A. Stone]

Rival 4-6-0s meet in the ex-G.W.R. station at Dorchester (West), February 1959. 'King Arthur' No. 30770 *Sir Prianius* is at the head of a Weymouth to Dorchester local, while modified 'Hall' No. 7917 *North Aston Hall* powers a Bristol to Weymouth stopper.

[Derek Cross]

The ex-L.S.W.R. station, Dorchester (South), was one of the delightful oddities inherited by BR. Down trains simply called at the platform alongside the track, but up trains from Weymouth had to reverse into the terminus shown here. No doubt the operating authorities are glad that a new platform has been built to obviate this awkward movement. No. 35028 *Clan Line* is about to leave with the 9.21 a.m. Weymouth to Waterloo, 23 May 1964.

[J. R. Besley]

Modified 'Battle of Britain' Pacific No. 34056 *Croydon* is seen approaching Dorchester (South) with the 8.25 a.m. Waterloo to Weymouth, 17 September 1966. The L.S.W.R. and Southern Railway maintained a small shed at Dorchester with some dozen engines allocated, but the duties were transferred to Weymouth in the 1950s.   [D. T. Cobbe]

Grimy Pacific No. 34087 *145 Squadron* approaching Wool with the 9.49 a.m. Weymouth to Waterloo on 25 July 1965.
                                                                                                    [W. L. Underhay]

The Saturday morning through train to Waterloo leaves Swanage behind No. 34005 *Barnstaple* on 8 September 1956. The engine is still largely in its original form, the few modifications include the extended smoke deflectors, angled cab spectacles and the removal of the side sheeting between the cylinders and buffer beam. As the 'West Countries' were notorious for slipping, it is noteworthy that the driver is using the steam sanders to gain adhesion, even on the level start out of the station.

[G. D. King]

Almost ten years later, in August 1966, No. 34005 *Barnstaple* is again on view at Swanage, ready to head the Waterloo train. In the meantime the engine has undergone the complete modification as conceived by R. G. Jarvis in 1957. The most obvious change is the conventional outline of the unstreamlined locomotive, but of greater significance is the appearance of the normal Walschaerts valve gear in place of the previously invisible Bulleid arrangement in its oil-bath between the frames. The shaft from the reversing wheel also betrays the change in this gear from the inaccurate steam operated controls on the original engine. Ivatt Class '2' No. 41230 is working the local service from Wareham.

[G. D. King]

Drummond 'M7' 0-4-4T No. 30111
leaves Swanage with its rake of
L.S.W.R. coaches in the evening of 25
August 1956. The ten mile branch
from Worgret Junction (a mile west of
the market town of Wareham) was
opened on 20 May 1885, with one
intermediate station at Corfe Castle.
An engine for the branch train was
stabled overnight in the small shed
seen on the left.   [G. D. King]

No. 30111 again, shunting stock in the
summer sunshine at Swanage, 27
August 1956. The branch line tank
was subshedded here, from its parent
depot of Bournemouth, until the
service was dieselised in September
1966.   [G. D. King]

During the summer months, several trains arrived at Swanage from various centres. No. 31633, one of Maunsell's 'U' Class 2-6-0s of 1927, is seen arriving at the attractive Dorset resort with a train from Basingstoke, 27 August 1956. These 6ft. Moguls were ideal motive power for such turns.

[G. D. King]

The Bournemouth to Brockenhurst trains also passed through Wimborne. Motor-fitted 'M7' No. 30056 starts away towards Bournemouth with its light load on 17 August 1962.
[M. J. Fox]

Following the construction of the line from Alderbury Junction, near Salisbury, to West Moors, in December 1866, cross country trains were run from Salisbury to Bournemouth. The service continued until 4 May 1964, when that nineteen-mile section was closed. 'U' Class No. 31632 makes a brisk start out of Wimborne with the 9.23 a.m. from Salisbury to Bournemouth on 21 December 1963.
[M. J. Fox]

One of the popular Standard Class '4' 2-6-0s, No. 76019, at Holes Bay Junction with a Templecombe to Bournemouth (West) local on 25 August 1964. The train has come off the Somerset and Dorset tracks at Broadstone, a mile or so up the line. The double track curving away to the left leads through Hamworthy Junction and on to Weymouth.
[W. L. Underhay]

Drummond 'M7' 0-4-4T
No. 30108 of Bournemouth
shed propels its two-
coach set out of Poole,
working on the
Bournemouth to
Brockenhurst service.
The driver is in the front
compartment of the train,
leaving the firemen on
the footplate to see to
the fire and water supply
to the boiler. This push-
and-pull arrangement
avoided the need for
running round at the end
of each trip.
    [G. A. Richardson]

The large Standard Class '5' 4-6-0s were very popular with the Southern enginemen. With 6ft. 2in. wheels and a well-designed front-end, these engines were speedy machines and the Southern men enjoyed driving them hard. No. 73080 *Merlin* coasts around the curve into Poole with the 8.30 a.m. from Waterloo on 25 August 1964. [W. L. Underhay]

Standard Mogul No. 76008 tackles the 1 in 60 from Poole up to Parkstone with an up stopping train, 13 October 1961. These 2-6-0s, with 5ft. 3in. wheels, were useful replacements for the veteran Drummond types which were withdrawn in the 1950s.

[G. A. Richardson]

The headcode on 'N' Class 2-6-0 No. 31841 denotes that this train is a Bournemouth (West) to Salisbury service. The scene is Parkstone, on 31 March 1962.

[M. J. Fox]

Heavy expresses required help on the severe 1 in 50/60 climb up Parkstone bank. Standard Class '4' 2-6-4T No. 80138 provides powerful rear-end assistance to the 9.25 a.m. from Weymouth as the train hammers through Parkstone station on 20 August 1966.

[W. L. Underhay]

Yet another Standard class at work in the Bournemouth area, this time one of the Class '4' 4-6-0s, several of which were allocated to Eastleigh shed at the period. Double-chimney No. 75067 rolls down the grade through Parkstone with a freight on 25 August 1964. With their 5ft. 8in. wheels, these 4-6-0s were virtually tender versions of the Class '4' tanks, of which No. 80138 on the previous page is an example.   [W. L. Underhay]

The terminus at Bournemouth (West) was opened on 15 June 1874. Several trains for London originated here, the most famous being the all-Pullman 'Bournemouth Belle', which makes a fine sight as it departs behind Nine Elms 'Merchant Navy' Pacific No. 35015 *Rotterdam Lloyd* on 31 March 1962. No. 30127 on the left is acting as station pilot, No. 76016 heads a Salisbury train, while another Standard has steam up for a tender-first run to Brockenhurst.   [M. J. Fox]

The West and Central stations at Bournemouth were connected by a short line opened in March 1888. On 9 September 1960 Eastleigh shed's 'Nelson' No. 30857 *Lord Howe* works the 11.30 a.m. from Waterloo along this line, which branches off the main Weymouth route at Gasworks Junction.   [D. T. Cobbe]

The Somerset and Dorset line trains used the West station at Bournemouth. For many years, the famous 'Pines Express' headed away from the terminus, and over the mountainous Mendip route, while lesser trains ran to Bath and Bristol. No. 76019 simmers quietly at the head of the 1.10 p.m. to Bristol, 25 August 1964. The station was closed in October 1965.   [W. L. Underhay]

The fireman has put the dart into the fire on No. 34042 *Dorchester* as the light Pacific stands at the head of an up express in Bournemouth (Central) station, in 1962. This through station was opened in 1883 and became the principal station in the rapidly expanding resort.

[G. A. Richardson]

Standard Class '4' 2-6-4T No. 80040 comes off at Bournemouth (Central) after working its roster on an up train from Weymouth, while rebuilt 'West Country' No. 34009 *Lyme Regis* blows off at 250lbs. per sq. in. as she waits to take the fast on to Waterloo in the autumn of 1962.

48

[G. A. Richardson]

The 6ft. 2in. driving wheels of 150-ton Rebuilt 'Merchant Navy' Pacific No. 35024 *East Asiatic Company* make their first tentative revolutions at the start of the 108-mile run home to London as this Nine Elms locomotive heads an up express out of Bournemouth (Central) on 27 September 1962.   [G. A. Richardson]

Remanning a 'West Country' at Bournemouth (Central) on a foggy winter morning in 1962. The fireman is making certain that the tank is full, while his driver has a brief word with a colleague. There was nothing worse for footplatemen than a run to London in a real 'pea-souper', especially with a streamlined Bulleid, as the steam drifted around the cab windows, and mingling with the fog made the numerous signals almost invisible.   [G. A. Richardson]   51

Rebuilt 'Merchant Navy' Pacific No. 35026 *Langport and Holt Line* indulges in a spectacular bout of slipping when restarting a down express at Brockenhurst, 13 May 1966. The Bulleids in their original condition were extremely light-footed; after rebuilding they were a little better, as there was no oil to be flung out of leaking oil-baths, but careful handling was absolutely essential in order to make a clean get-away. The stiff pull-out regulator handle wasn't much help in this respect! However, once these powerful machines were on the move, they really could go, and many instances of 100 m.p.h. running were recorded in the final years of steam operation.

[D. M. Cox]

The verdant greenery of the New Forest in early summer is hardly matched by the filthy Brunswick green of 'Merchant Navy' 4-6-2 No. 35029 *Ellerman Lines,* which is working an express from Bournemouth up to Oxford and points north on 22 May 1965. The express trains on the Bournemouth line were often hauled by similarly grimy-looking locomotives in the latter days of steam, yet wonderful performances were often obtained in spite of the general neglect of the motive power.

[D. M. Cox]

The four-mile branch to Lymington was opened in 1858, and the extension to the Pier was completed in 1884. For many years the branch trains were in the capable hands of the Drummond 'M7' tanks. No. 30029 is propelling its train across the harbour on 6 June 1962.

[M. J. Fox]

Lymington Pier station, 14 July 1960, with 'M7' No. 30480 standing at the platform, and the Freshwater ferry waiting alongside the Pier. This alternate route to the Isle of Wight helps to relieve congestion on the Portsmouth to Ryde services.

[H. C. Casserley]

A Standard Class '3' 2-6-2 tank barks away from Ringwood with the 11.4 a.m. Brockenhurst to Bournemouth (Central), 25 April 1964. These medium-sized tanks had replaced the ageing Drummonds on many local services in the Bournemouth area by this date. The original railhead for Bournemouth was at Christchurch, reached by the eight-mile line from Ringwood which, opened in 1862, ran from the bay platform under the overall roof seen on the right.

[M. J. Fox]

A study of a 'Merchant Navy' action near Christchurch, heading an up express to Waterloo. These large Pacifics had a certain functional elegance about their appearance following the drastic rebuilding authorised by the BR locomotive authorities and they would have had many more years of useful service in front of them if the decision to abandon steam had not been implemented in July 1967.

[G. A. Richardson]

Many of Maunsell's 'N' Class 2-6-0s were erected in Woolwich Arsenal in the early 1920s and were ever after known as 'Woolworths'. Like the products from their famous namesake, they were excellent value for money, being useful medium-power mixed traffic locomotives. No. 31815 heads a freight down the main line at Brockenhurst on 9 August 1961.   [D. T. Cobbe]

Maunsell's 'U' Class 2-6-0s were very similar to the 'Ns' but had 6ft. driving wheels instead of the 5ft. 6in. driving wheels of the 'Woolworths'. No. 31800 is working the 4.12 p.m. from Southampton Terminus past Ashurst (near Lyndhurst Road) on 2 June 1965.
[D. M. Cox]

The nine-mile branch from the main line at Totton down to Fawley was opened as recently as 1925. Intermediate stations were provided at Marchwood and Hythe. No. 30127 is seen at the former location with the 4.50 p.m. Fawley to Southampton Central on 9 August 1961. The 'M7s' originally had a coal capacity of three tons, but this was increased by 5cwt. by the addition of the coal rails above the bunker.

[D. T. Cobbe]

No. 30127 has arrived at Fawley with the 3.0 p.m. from Eastleigh on 9 August 1961. The main reason for the construction of the branch can be seen in the background—the Esso petrol tanks. The vast oil refinery which has been built on the west bank of South-ampton Water brings in super-tankers from the Middle East, and the Southern Region obtains a great deal of revenue from the oil trains which leave the branch daily for numerous destinations. The passenger service was withdrawn on 11 February 1966.

[D. T. Cobbe]

The fireman is busy shovelling coal on 'N' Class No. 31408 as the Mogul prepares to leave Totton with the 4.12 p.m. from Southampton Terminus, 11 August 1965. [D. M. Cox]

During the summer of 1964, a Feltham 'S15' 4-6-0 was rostered to the 5.10 p.m. Southampton Terminus to Bournemouth (Central) stopper. No. 30843 has the turn on 2 July and is seen pulling away from Totton. The large wheel in the signal box operates the level crossing gates.

[D. M. Cox]

Although the names
were omitted when the
'K' Class tanks were
rebuilt into 'U' Class
2-6-0s in 1927, the Nos.
31790 to 31809 locomotives
remained 'Rivers' to the
men. The original engine,
No. 31790, seen at Totton,
has the 4.12 p.m. from
Southampton Terminus
on 12 April 1965.
[D. M. Cox]

'Q1' No. 33027 heads t
5.10 p.m. from
Southampton Termin
out of Lyndhurst Road
place of the usual 'S1
on 21 August 1964.
Although designed as
freight engines, these
Bulleid products revea
a very good turn of
speed when the chanc
arose.   [M. J. F

Bulleid's modificatio
the cylinders and bla
pipe of Maunsell's 'L
Nelson' design impr
the performance of th
class considerably. T
large diameter chimn
and the high-sided
tender also improved
looks of these alread
handsome machines.
No. 30854 *Howard of
Effingham* approache
Southampton (Centra
with the 2.20 p.m.
Bournemouth (West)
Waterloo, 26 July 194
[D. T. Co

'Battle of Britain' 4-6-2 No. 34071 *601 Squadron* hurries the 'Pines Express' away from Southampton (Central) on 8 March 1965. The train was running about thirty minutes late, and the crew had snatched several hundred gallons of water during the stop, but had no time to screw the water-column valve home tight!

[D. M. Cox]

As No. 34071 and the 'Pines' disappear around the curve, No. 31408 follows with the 4.12 p.m. from the terminus. It will be noticed that the express has the distant signal for Millbrook, the next station down the line, in the off position, whereas the stopper will be halted there, because the two down tracks merge into one line just west of that station.

[D. M. Cox]

Locomotive men have always been acquainted with the realities of 'unsocial hours', for many of their turns of duty took place under cover of darkness. The crew of Rebuilt 'West Country' No. 34034 *Honiton* take water at Southampton (Central) in the late evening of 15 October 1965.

[D. M. Cox]

Yet another view of the 4.12 p.m., this time at its point of origin, Southampton Terminus on 3 June 1965. 'U' Class Mogul No. 31800 of Eastleigh shed is backing extra stock on to its train before departure. The running lines on the left lead into the Old Docks, the cranes of which can be seen in the distance beyond the large block building.

[D. M. Cox]

An Old Docks scene, taken on 18 June 1965. For many years, the Adams 'B4' 0-4-0Ts worked on the sharply curved tracks in the Docks, but after the Second World War, the Southern purchased fourteen of these powerful 0-6-0 tanks from the U.S. Army. They proved extremely popular with the men, having a large, comfortable cab, easily accessible motion and above all, plenty of power for hauling heavy rakes of wagons or coaching stock. [D. M. Cox]

Maunsell 'S15' 4-6-0 No. 30824 storms through St. Denys with a special freight from the nearby Bevois Park yard on 28 June 1965. The fireman is looking back along the train awaiting the hand signal from the guard that all is well. A small shed existed in the Docks for the local tanks, but engines for these main-line turns from Southampton were serviced at Eastleigh, six miles away.

[M. J. Fox]

Another Maunsell mixed-traffic engine, 'U' Class 2-6-0 No. 31637, sets out from Eastleigh in the bleak mid-winter. The engine is seen passing Eastleigh South Junction with a goods for Fratton (Portsmouth), on 30 January 1954.

[L. Elsey]

An Andover to Southampton local, composed of ex-L.S.W.R. stock, pauses in the afternoon sunshine at Eastleigh on 2 July 1954. The train engine is Drummond '700' Class 0-6-0 No. 30306. These locomotives were introduced as a heavy goods class in 1897, and achieved considerable success in this role. Drummond's successor, Robert Urie, was an advocate of superheating and when modernising the design after the Great War he introduced this improvement along with the stovepipe chimney. The modified engines continued in service until the early 1960s appearing on light passenger turns such as this one on occasions. These austere 0-6-0s were always known as 'Black Motors' to the footplate crews who handled them for over sixty years.

[Brian Morrison]

The L.S.W.R. opened its new locomotive works at Eastleigh in 1910. At the time this had the most up-to-date facilities in the country and throughout the steam era it remained to the fore as a principal locomotive works for British Railways. Rebuilt 'West Country' No. 34025 *Whimple* undergoes a general repair in the erecting shop, in company with No. 34071 *601 Squadron* on 16 January 1966.

[N. E. Preedy]

The 'Merchant Navy' Pacifics were always associated with Eastleigh Works. No. 35017 *Belgian Marine* is half-way through a 'heavy general' 1 May 1965. The unique Bulleid-Firth-Brown driving wheels of the Pacific stand fully revealed alongside the stripped-down locomotive.

[D. M. Cox]

Drummond's 'T9' 4-4-0s were successful express passenger engines. Following Urie's modifications, which included superheating, they became outstanding engines. Reliable, and extremely free-running, these old ladies continued in service until the early 1960s. No. 30117, seen passing Eastleigh with empty stock on 2 July 1954, amassed nearly two million miles of running before its withdrawal in July 1961.

[Brian Morrison]

The driver of No. 35021 *New Zealand Line* has shut off steam for a steady run through Eastleigh with a down express, 24 March 1965.
Below: the winter air causes the exhaust to hang heavily around the smokebox of Rebuilt 'West Country' No. 34047 *Callington* which is seen passing Shawford, some five miles north of Eastleigh, on 15 January 1966.

[D. M. Cox]

The Didcot, Newbury and Southampton Railway was one of those small companies which blossomed in the late nineteenth century and had high hopes of becoming vital cross-country routes. From Grouping until 1948 it was largely worked by G.W.R. engines but Southern types appeared in later years. 'T9' No. 30707 has worked down from Newbury with ex-G.W.R. stock and has run on to the down Southern main line at Shawford, 15 June 1957.

[L. Elsey]

Winchester (City) is the main line station in the Hampshire city. No. 30028 is working the Winchester to Alton service, which will branch off the main line at Winchester Junction. The Ivatt Class '2' 2-6-2T No. 41293 was one of a series which arrived in the Eastleigh area to replace ageing Southern power.

[Stanley Creer]

'T9' 4-4-0 No. 30288 stands in the station at Winchester (Chesil) on 2 June 1956. Opened in May 1885, this was the original terminus of the D.N.S.R., but it attracted little traffic and in October 1891 the connection with the L.S.W.R. main line was made at Shawford Junction. Passenger services south of Newbury were withdrawn in March 1960.

[A. E. Bennett]

'Battle of Britain' 4-6-2 No. 34052 *Lord Dowding,* not up to the usual Salisbury standards of cleanliness, stands at the head of the 10.0 a.m. from Salisbury to Waterloo in Andover Junction station on 12 March 1965.

[D. T. Cobbe]

Drummond '700' Class 0-6-0 No. 30317 gently accelerates away from Newton Tony with a single coach towards its destination Bulford on 11 June 1952, a week before the branch passenger service from Salisbury was withdrawn. The line to Amesbury was opened in 1902, Bulford being reached in 1906. The branch was very busy during both World Wars, and heavy trains continued to carry servicemen to and from London (Waterloo) until the 1960s. 'U' Class Moguls hauled many of these fasts, although Bulleid light Pacifics were also permitted and appeared regularly.

[A. C. V. Kendall]

Urie 'N15' 4-6-0 No. 30740 *Merlin* tops the summit of the climb up from Andover Junction as it roars through Grateley on 29 September 1951. At the time the engine was allocated to Bournemouth (71B) shed and was a stranger on the line to Salisbury. The electric headlamps serve as a reminder that this engine was one of those modified in the abortive post-war oil-fired conversion programme on the SR. [Brian A. Butt]

The driver of 'West Country' 4-6-2 No. 34047 *Callington* peers ahead to catch a glimpse of Salisbury inner home signal which stands a few hundred yards ahead. The train, seen on 12 March 1965, is the 10.54 a.m. from Waterloo, one of the series of semi-fasts which left the capital at 54 minutes past the hour for the Basingstoke and Salisbury route. These trains, running to Woking and then calling at all stations to Salisbury, were difficult trains to time with the Bulleid Pacifics which were so prone to slipping.

[D. T. Cobbe]

The splendid Pacific No. 35007 *Aberdeen Commonwealth* spent over twenty years at Salisbury shed. The engine is on one of its regular rosters—the 8.15 a.m. to Waterloo and down with the 1.0 p.m. with a Salisbury crew and then on to Exeter with the Exmouth Junction man seen here, pulling out of Salisbury on 23 October 1963. He had come up to Salisbury with the 10.30 a.m. from Exeter earlier in the day. Behind the busy West Box is Salisbury locomotive depot.

[K. A. Stone]

Yeovil (72C) shed had a stud of 'U' Class Moguls for many years. One of these, No. 31798, stands in Salisbury station after working a train from Bournemouth. The flat-sided tender attached to the 2-6-0 has a capacity of five tons of coal and 3500 gallons of water.

[K. A. Stone]

Maunsell 'S15' 4-6-0 No. 30840 from Feltham (70B) shed spent most of its life on heavy goods turns in South-West England, but on the Saturday morning of 7 December 1963, it is ready to work an up van train away from Salisbury to London. The ensemble which had been shunted by ex-G.W.R. pannier No. 4626, stands in No. 6 platform at Salisbury, the bay from which the Bournemouth and Portsmouth locals usually departed. [D. M. Cox]

Salisbury shed first acquired Bulleid Pacifics in 1941, the year in which the 'Merchant Navy' Class was introduced. Bulleids were still on its books when steam operations ceased in July 1967. A trio of Rebuilds stand inside the ten-road building in the mid-1960s. No. 34056 *Croydon* and No. 34071 *601 Squadron* have been prepared for their next duty, while the 'Battle of Britain' in No. 10 road on the right is undergoing a 'periodical examination' to the cylinders and valves.

[D. M. Cox]

When Lawson Billinton's seven 'L' Class 4-6-4 tanks were rendered redundant by electrification in the early 'thirties, Maunsell rebuilt them into these handsome 4-6-0s. They were classified 'N15X' and it was assumed that they would supplement the stud of 'King Arthurs', but the Western Section men never really took to them and they were relegated to such duties as the 2.48 p.m. from Basingstoke which is seen entering Salisbury behind No. 32327 *Trevithick* on 26 August 1948.

[D. T. Cobbe]

The 'top end' of Salisbury station, 22 January 1962. No. 35003 *Royal Mail* has worked the 8.25 a.m. ex-Plymouth from Exeter with an Exmouth Junction Top Link crew, who are now being relieved by footplatemen of Salisbury No. 2 (Mixed Traffic) Link. The firemen are busy on the tender taking water and shovelling the coal forward. Another pair of Salisbury men, of No. 1 ('Main Line') Link are nearing the end of their day's work as they ease into the station on No. 35001 *Channel Packet* at the head of the down 'A.C.E.' The notorious 10-chain curve which caused the disastrous derailment to 4-4-0 No. 421 on the fatal night of 30 June 1906 is prominent in the centre of the scene.

[G. A. Richardson]

The electric services from Waterloo to Portsmouth began running in July 1937, but steam appeared at the naval town for a further 25 years on trains on the non-electrified Reading, Salisbury and Bournemouth trains. 'T9' No. 30729 of Fratton shed backs out of Portsmouth and Southsea (Low Level) with the stock of a cross-country train on 25 May 1957.   [A. E. Bennett]

Apart from the BR lined-out black livery on the 'M7', this scene could well be in pre-Grouping days, as the ensemble is pure L.S.W.R. No. 30055 of Fratton (71D) shed is signalled away from Droxford on the Meon Valley line on 17 April 1954. This 22-mile route between Fareham and Alton was opened in 1903, but it never really prospered and services were withdrawn on 5 February 1955. [L. Elsey]

The Gosport line, opened in November 1841, was the original route from London to the Portsmouth area. Following the construction of the Portsmouth Direct line, the importance of the Gosport branch diminished, and the passenger services ceased on 8 June 1953. However, 'N' Class 2-6-0 No. 31411 had seven well-filled coaches behind the tender as it hauled a rail tour along the branch on 20 February 1966.

[D. M. Cox]

The four-and-a-half-mile line from Havant to Hayling Island was opened on 16 July 1867 and in its latter years was much-visited by enthusiasts as it was the home ground of several of the famous Brighton 'Terriers', the Stroudley 'A1Xs'. No. 32646, seen near Langston on 27 August 1959, was built in 1877 as No. 46 *Newington*. Sold to the L.S.W.R. (No. 734) in 1903, it worked on the Lyme Regis branch for some years until it migrated to the Isle of Wight in 1913, where it remained until 1949. Following its return to the mainland, No. 32646 worked from Fratton shed until its withdrawal in November 1963 when the Hayling Island services were abandoned. [G. D. King]

The severe weight restrictions imposed on Langston Viaduct ensured the longevity of the 'Terriers'. No. 32646 heads for the Island on 11 August 1963. [G. D. King] **Below:** another view of Langston Viaduct, with No. 32650 trailing black smoke into the August sky in 1961. [P. J. Lynch]

In order to allow the Civil Engineers more scope while electrification of the Bournemouth line was in progress, a number of fast were diverted via the Alton to Winchester line. Not for nothing was this switchback known as 'over the Alps', and many excellent photographs were obtained by skilled cameramen on the formidable 1 in 60 Medstead Bank; No. 34052, the then nameless *Lord Dowding* rouses the echoes with the down 10.30 a.m. to Weymouth on 18 September 1966.

[D. T. Cobbe

Although the passenger services to Portsmouth from London were electrified, the freight turns to 'Pompey' continued to be worked by steam power until the mid-1960s. No. 30513, seen passing Havant in 1959, was one of the twenty 'S15' mixed-traffic 4-6-0s introduced by Robert Urie in 1920. While not as free-running as the later Maunsell variants, never-the-less these engines were rugged, reliable motive power, and some men preferred them on the heaviest freight jobs when hard slogging was the order of the day.

[N. E. Preedy]

The mighty 'Nelson' 4-6-0
No. 30858 *Lord Duncan* looks
rather out of place on the
single line near Medstead when
diverted on to the Alton route
back in 1955.   [L. Elsey]

Bournemouth men knew the road as far north as Oxford and for many years had two daily turns, taking their own engines over the 'foreign' lines north of Basingstoke. The most usual classes involved were 'West Country' Pacifics or 'King Arthur' and 'Lord Nelson' 4-6-0s, but the Southern crew had a 'Remembrance' 4-6-0 No. 32327 *Trevithick* for the York to Bournemouth on 24 September 1955. No doubt these men were thinking harsh thoughts about this as they pull away southwards with the Gresley stock on the first leg of their long run home.   [G. D. King]